SRI LANKA

By Jagger Youssef and
Laura L. Sullivan

EXPLORING WORLD CULTURES

Cavendish Square

Published in 2027 by Cavendish Square Publishing, LLC
2544 Clinton Street, Buffalo, NY 14224

Second Edition

Website: cavendishsq.com

Cataloging-in-Publication Data

Names: Youssef, Jagger. | Sullivan, Laura L.
Title: Sri Lanka / Jagger Youssef and Laura L. Sullivan.
Description: Second edition. | Buffalo, NY : Cavendish Square Publishing, 2027. | Series: Exploring world cultures | Includes glossary and index.
Identifiers: ISBN 9781502677013 (pbk.) | ISBN 9781502677020 (library bound) | ISBN 9781502677037 (ebook)
Subjects: LCSH: Sri Lanka--Juvenile literature.
Classification: LCC DS489.Y68 2027 | DDC 954.93--dc23

Writers: Jagger Youssef; Laura L. Sullivan (second edition)
Editor: Therese Shea
Designer: Deanna Lepovich

The photographs in this book are used by permission and through the courtesy of: Cover Jaromir Chalabala/Shutterstock.com; p. 4 alonanola/Shutterstock.com; p. 5 trabantos/Shutterstock.com; p. 6 Peter Hermes Furian/Shutterstock.com; p. 7 Travel Faery/Shutterstock.com; p. 8 1880s Sorting tea Ceylon Sri Lanka 2/Wikimedia Commons; pp. 9, 25 (top) Ruwan Walpola/Shutterstock.com; p. 10 Anura Kumara Dissanayake in 2025/Wikimedia Commons; p. 11 Xandra R/Shutterstock.com; p. 11 (inset) Thilanka Sadaruwan/Shutterstock.com; p. 12 Melinda Nagy/Shutterstock.com; p. 13 Easy Capture Images/Shutterstock.com; p. 14 Saranga/Shutterstock.com; p. 15 kingma photos/Shutterstock.com; p. 16 SamanWeeratunga/Shutterstock.com; p. 17 Jon Chica/Shutterstock.com; p. 19 (top) goran_safarek/Shutterstock.com; p. 19 (bottom) Rawpixel.com/Shutterstock.com; p. 20 Kurka Geza Corey/Shutterstock.com; p. 21 Nuwanga Rajapaksha/Shutterstock.com; p. 22 Nilanka Sampath/Shutterstock.com; p. 23 Zysko Sergii/Shutterstock.com; p. 25 (bottom) Nadee photography/Shutterstock.com; p. 26 Try_my_best/Shutterstock.com; p. 27 Sergii Figurnyi/Shutterstock.com; p. 28 Siyapath/Shutterstock.com; p. 29 Leon Concept/Shutterstock.com.

CPSIA compliance information: Batch #CS27CSQ: For further information contact Cavendish Square Publishing LLC at 1-877-980-4450.

Printed in United States of America

CONTENTS

INTRODUCTION

Sri Lanka is a South Asian nation with a long and interesting history. Different people of different cultures, or ways of life, have made the country their home over the years. Sometimes cultures clashed. A **civil war** broke out there in 1983 and lasted until 2009. Today, the country is still recovering from that time of fighting. Many people are still poor. Many must grow their own food. The country is in **debt** to other countries too.

Sri Lanka's capital city is Sri Jayawardenepura Kotte. However, Colombo, shown here, is the largest city and the center of business activity.

But Sri Lanka has a lot of bright spots. It has beautiful beaches, lush forests, and stunning mountains. In fact, the land was given the name "the Pearl of the Indian Ocean" for its beauty. Sri Lanka also has beautiful temples and other places of worship. It has cities with good food and exciting events. Many people around the world visit Sri Lanka each year. The Sri Lankan government hopes more visitors will bring money and business into the country. This would help improve life for all Sri Lankans.

Most Sri Lankans live in rural, or countryside, areas.

GEOGRAPHY

Sri Lanka is an island country in the Indian Ocean. It's south of India. There was a natural land bridge between Sri Lanka and India at one time. However, it's not there anymore. Now the countries are separated by the bodies of water called the Gulf of Mannar and the Palk Strait.

FACT!
Sri Lanka is usually hot, but in the mountains it can get cold.

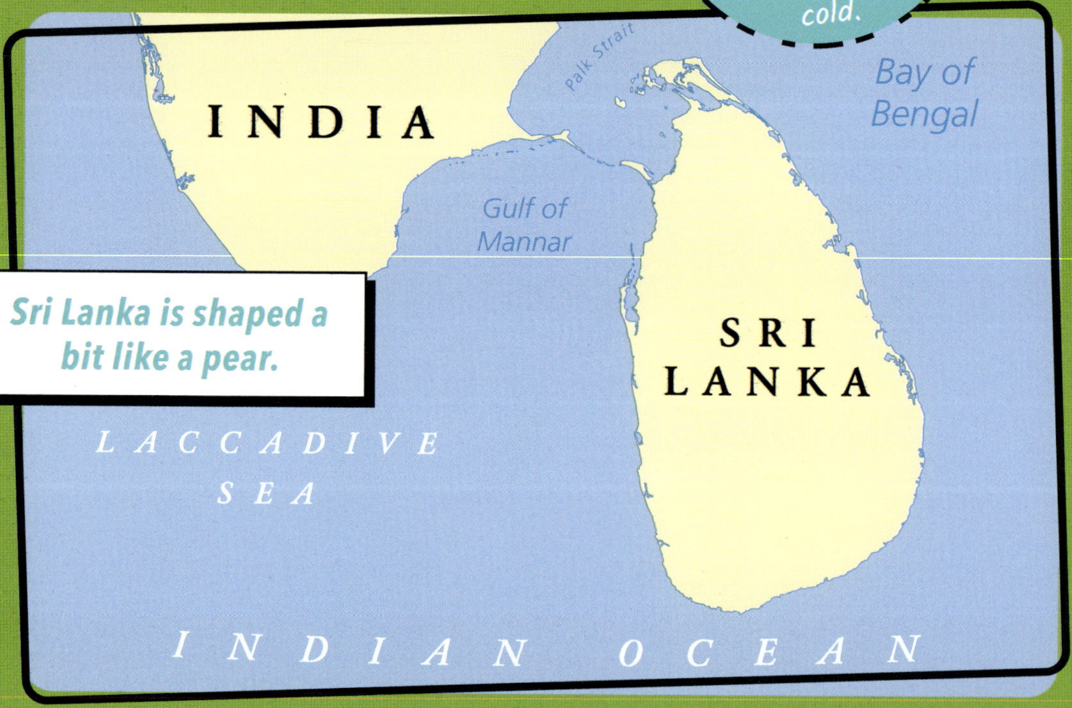

Sri Lanka is shaped a bit like a pear.

Sri Lanka has long coastlines. Mangrove trees grow along the coast. These trees help protect the inner island from **hurricanes** and giant ocean waves called tsunamis. Sri Lanka has more than 100 rivers. Many of these rivers have beautiful waterfalls.

The weather in Sri Lanka is warm and wet. It has two **monsoon** seasons, which bring heavy rains to different parts of the country.

Mangrove trees grow in salt water.

MANY MOUNTAINS

Sri Lanka's mountainous area is in the south-central part of the country. The highest point is a mountain called Pidurutalagala. It's 8,281 feet (2,524 meters) tall.

HISTORY

Sri Lankan **civilizations** go back more than 2,000 years. Sri Lankan kingdoms traded spices such as cinnamon with the Roman Empire and Europe in the Middle Ages.

This is a photo of a worker sorting tea in Ceylon (today's Sri Lanka) in the late 1800s.

BEGINNINGS

The first people on Sri Lanka were likely the Vedda people. Around the 400s BCE, they began to mix with settlers from India, who are now known as the Sinhalese.

Later, Europeans took over the island. The Portuguese controlled the country during the 1600s. Then the Dutch ruled during the 1700s. The British took over in 1796 and called the island Ceylon. The Sri Lankan people wanted freedom from the British. The country became independent, or free, in 1948. However, the British government had some power over it until 1972.

During the civil war from 1983 to 2009, a group called the Tamil Tigers fought for an independent Tamil country. They didn't win. Tens of thousands of people died.

FACT!

Both the Sinhalese and Tamil peoples of Sri Lanka trace their roots to people who came from India.

People look at a war monument, which lists names of those who died during the Sri Lankan civil war.

GOVERNMENT

Sri Lanka is Asia's oldest **democratic republic**. Its people have had voting rights since 1931. Under the constitution of 1978, the country's highest law, Sri Lankan government has three parts: executive, legislative, and judicial. The president leads the executive part. They serve for five years. They also name their advisors called cabinet ministers.

FACT!
The Sri Lankan president oversees the army, navy, and air force.

The Sri Lankan president is elected directly by the people. Anura Kumara Dissanayake has been president since 2024.

The Presidential Secretariat (above) is the office of the president. The parliament building is shown to the left.

The parliament, more than 200 people, makes up the legislative part. Members of the parliament are also elected for five-year terms. They make the country's laws. The parliament is headed by a prime minister, who is selected by the president.

Finally, the judicial part includes the Supreme Court, the Appeals Court, and several lower courts. The Vedda people have some of their own laws, however.

A FIRST

Sirimavo Bandaranaike of Sri Lanka became the world's first female prime minister in 1960. She was elected after her husband, Prime Minister S.W.R.D. Bandaranaike, was killed.

THE ECONOMY

Like most countries with a long history, Sri Lanka has an **economy** that has changed over time. At first, farming was most important to Sri Lanka. Until the mid-1800s, large farms called plantations grew many crops. Tea, rubber, coconut, and cinnamon were sold around the world. They helped Sri Lanka earn money. These crops are still grown today, but farming isn't as important to the economy overall. Factories in Sri Lanka create food products or make clothing.

FACT!

Sri Lanka is the second biggest **exporter** of tea, after China.

Over 1 million people work in the tea industry in Sri Lanka.

The Sri Lankan economy struggled for many years. Today, it's improving. More people are making more money. Most homes have electricity and running water. Other countries are helping Sri Lanka's economy grow. The United States and China are Sri Lanka's biggest trade partners. This means these countries send many goods to and receive many goods from Sri Lanka.

Many of the major companies of Sri Lanka have headquarters in the city of Colombo.

TOURISM

Tourism is the business of bringing travelers into a country. It's one of the growing parts of the Sri Lankan economy. The island is often on lists of the best places to visit.

THE ENVIRONMENT

Sri Lanka's many animals include leopards, elephants, and monkeys. These animals depend on the country's wild, natural places to live. National parks and **nature preserves** have been set aside in Sri Lanka.

Sri Lanka has a lot of forests. However, people want to cut the forests down because wood is valuable. It can make houses and other goods. People use wood for heat and cooking fuel as well. Along the coast, shrimp farming threatens mangrove trees. Shrimp farms also harm coral reefs in the sea.

The Sri Lankan sloth bear has lost some of its natural home because of the clearing of forests for building and tea farms.

Today, many Sri Lankans drive cars and trucks. These machines cause a lot of air pollution. In the countryside, people litter and make the land and water dirty. The government plans to move away from using polluting fuels in the coming years.

FACT!

Sri Lanka has banned the use of kinds of plastics that can be bad for nature.

In Sri Lanka, some elephants are wild, and some elephants are used to do work for people.

MAINTAINING THE MANGROVES

Sri Lanka is a world leader in mangrove tree protection. The people there understand how important these trees are for guarding the coast and helping wildlife.

THE PEOPLE TODAY

About 22 million people live in Sri Lanka. It's a densely populated country, which means people live closely together. Most people live near the city of Colombo.

Different **ethnic** groups live in Sri Lanka. The Sinhalese make up nearly 75 percent of the population. They mostly live in the central and southwest parts of the country.

Sri Lankan Tamils make up about 12 percent of the population. They mostly live in the north and east of the country.

FACT!

Indian Tamils were brought over to Sri Lanka by the British to work on tea farms.

Young Tamil students walk to school in Sri Lanka.

Sri Lankan Moors are another group. They make up about 10 percent of all Sri Lankans. Tamils from India and Malaysia also live on the island. Sri Lankan **descendants** of people who came from Europe are called Burghers. There are also a small group of Chinese, as well as Africans who are called Kaffirs.

Different ethnic groups mix in the cities of Sri Lanka.

THE VEDDA

Less than 1 percent of the Sri Lankan population are Vedda, who are descendants of the first people that lived on the island. Efforts are being made to save their culture.

LIFESTYLE

In Sri Lanka, family is important. Often, several **generations** live together. The father or the oldest son is often the head of the family. Grandparents and other elderly people live with family members. They're respected and help take care of the children.

Education is also important in Sri Lanka. More than 92 percent of adults and 98 percent of children know how to read. These are some of the highest numbers in South Asia. Education is free. Children have to go to school for at least thirteen years.

In the past, men were the leaders and workers, while women stayed at home with the children. Today, more women are working. However, women are still expected to take on most of the housework and child raising.

COMMUNITY CONCERNS

In villages in Sri Lanka, it's important to respect neighbors and provide help when they need it.

Visitors to Sri Lanka find most people to be welcoming.

FACT!

Younger people in Sri Lanka may address older people as "aunty" or "uncle."

When people visit each other in Sri Lanka, they're offered a drink or a meal.

RELIGION

People in Sri Lanka can practice any religion they want. This right is protected by their constitution. However, Buddhism is given a place of importance above others. Around 70 percent of Sri Lankans are Buddhist. They follow the teachings of the Buddha. The Buddha was a monk who wanted to help end suffering. Most Sinhalese are Buddhist.

About 13 percent of Sri Lankans are Hindu. Most of them are Tamil.

This is the inside of the Buddhist Temple of the Tooth in Kandy, Sri Lanka. It was built to house a tooth of the Buddha.

Islam came to Sri Lanka with Middle Eastern traders. Followers of Islam are called Muslims. Less than 10 percent of Sri Lankans are Muslim.

Europeans brought Christianity to Sri Lanka. Today, just about 7 percent of Sri Lankans are Christians.

FACT!

Most Sri Lankans say their religious beliefs are an important part of their everyday life.

This is a Hindu temple on the island of Nainativu, Sri Lanka.

HINDUISM

Hinduism is the third oldest religion in the world. Most Hindus worship one supreme being, Brahman, and believe in other forms of this being as well.

LANGUAGE

Sri Lanka has two official languages: Sinhalese and Tamil. More than 90 percent of Sri Lankans speak Sinhalese. Sinhalese has one of the largest alphabets, with as many as fifty-eight letters according to some. (Not all letters are in common use.) The Tamil language, spoken by about 20 percent of the country, has eighteen consonants and twelve vowels. Both Sinhalese and Tamil are used in schools.

FACT!

Tamil is also spoken in India, Singapore, and other countries.

In this sign, Sinhalese appears on top, Tamil in the middle, and English on the bottom.

English is also spoken in Sri Lanka. It's often used for business. About 20 percent of Sri Lankans speak English well. These people mostly live in cities.

There are also languages in Sri Lanka that mix two or more languages. They are called creoles. Two examples are Sri Lankan Malay Creole and Sri Lankan Portuguese Creole.

Sri Lankan rupees, or bank notes, have the three most used languages on them.

ENDANGERED LANGUAGE

Just a few hundred people speak the Vedda language. It's in danger of dying out.

ARTS AND FESTIVALS

Sri Lanka's rich cultures celebrate events throughout the year. Buddhists and Hindus celebrate the new year in April. In July and August, Buddhists celebrate the Festival of the Tooth. Dancers perform with whips and fire. Elephants are painted. They wear jewels and colorful fabrics.

In January, Tamils have a four-day festival thanking the sun god. In February or March, a festival honors the god of destruction and change, Shiva.

Sri Lankans keep arts alive too, such as special dances. Some dancers wear big headdresses. Other dances are less formal. Drums are used in most dances and plays.

Early plays started out as small shows in villages. After Sri Lanka became an independent nation, larger theaters were built for more people to see Sri Lankan plays.

MUSIC

The music of Sri Lanka has roots in Vedda, Hindu, Buddhist, European, and Indian history and culture.

Kandyan dance is the national dance. It's usually performed by male dancers.

FACT! Deepavali is the Hindu Festival of Lights in Sri Lanka.

This is the Sarachchandra Open-Air Theater. It's located at the University of Peradeniya in Central Sri Lanka.

FUN AND PLAY

Sri Lankans enjoy playing and watching sports. Cricket is the most popular sport. It's played with a ball and a bat. The men's national team won the Cricket World Cup in 1996 and went to the finals in 2007 and 2011.

Tennis, soccer, rugby, and track and field are also high-interest sports in Sri Lanka. The country has won two Olympic medals. In 1948, Duncan White won a silver medal for the men's 400-meter hurdles. Susanthika Jayasinghe won a silver medal for the women's 200-meter race in 2000.

Volleyball is the national sport of Sri Lanka.

Sri Lanka has two native forms of martial arts. They are called cheena di and angampora. Cheena di is a fighting style that may have come from Chinese monks hundreds of years ago. Angampora is a type of hand-to-hand combat that may be thousands of years old.

FACT!

Fishing using stilts began in Sri Lanka during World War II. It's still practiced in some places.

Stilt fishing, shown here, began because of a shortage of boats during World War II.

BANNED

Angampora was banned by the British when they controlled Sri Lanka. The ban was lifted in 2022, though Sri Lankans kept the tradition alive before this.

FOOD

Sri Lankan food reflects the many cultures that have called the island home throughout history. However, it's different than any other nation's food too. Sri Lankan dishes are known for using local food. This includes several kinds of rice. Coconut and seafood are part of many dishes as well. Rice dishes may be served with a curry, a spicy sauce.

Kokis *are made from rice flour and coconut milk.*

Sri Lankan cooks use many kinds of spices, giving their food lots of flavor. *Batu moju* is a curry with deep-fried eggplant and onion, green chili, and spices. *Kiribath* (or milk rice) is a Sri Lankan dish of rice cooked in coconut milk. It's cooled, cut, and eaten for the new year and other celebrations. Sri Lankan food is a delicious way to get to know more about this country.

FACT!

In Sri Lanka, sweet and salty snacks such as buns and rolls are called short eats or shorties.

Kiribath is cut into shapes, making it easy to hold and eat.

STREET FOOD

In Sri Lanka, snacks such as fried rice, egg rolls, and fish and vegetable wraps are sold on the streets for low cost.

GLOSSARY

civilization: Organized society with written records and laws.

civil war: A war between two groups within a country.

debt: Owing money to another person or group.

democratic republic: A government in which representatives are elected by the people.

descendant: A relative of someone from an earlier time.

economy: The money made in an area and how it is made.

ethnic: Having to do with a part of a person's identity based on where they or their family come from.

exporter: One who sends goods to be sold to another country.

generation: A group of individuals born about the same time.

Islam: The religious faith of Muslims including belief in Allah as the sole God and in Muhammad as his prophet.

monsoon: A seasonal change in wind direction resulting in a change in precipitation.

nature preserve: An area filled with plants and animals that is protected by the government.

stilt: A long pole used to elevate, or lift, buildings or people.

FIND OUT MORE

Books

Dickmann, Nancy. *Your Passport to Sri Lanka*. Oxford, UK: Raintree, 2022.

Pethiyagoda, Nanda, et al. *Sri Lanka*. Buffalo, NY: Cavendish Square Publishing, 2023.

Websites

Sri Lanka
www.ducksters.com/geography/country.php?country=Sri%20 Lanka
Review information about the geography, economy, and people of Sri Lanka on the Ducksters site.

Sri Lanka
kids.britannica.com/kids/article/Sri-Lanka/345789
Britannica Kids has the essential facts about this interesting country.

Video

Top Places to Visit in Sri Lanka with Kids
www.youtube.com/watch?v=GwSELDTO0H8
This video hits the highlights of Sri Lanka for a family to visit.

Publisher's note to educators and parents: Our editors have carefully reviewed these websites to ensure that they are suitable for students. Many websites change frequently, however, and we cannot guarantee that a site's future contents will continue to meet our high standards of quality and educational value. Be advised that students should be closely supervised whenever they access the internet.

INDEX